The Cold Book

Dr Mike Goldsmith
Miranda Smith

RED SHED

First published in Great Britain 2015 by Red Shed,
an imprint of Egmont UK Limited
The Yellow Building, 1 Nicholas Road,
London W11 4AN

www.egmont.co.uk

Text copyright © Egmont UK Limited 2015

ISBN 978 1 4052 7402 9

Consultancy by Dr Patricia Macnair and Ryan Marek.

A CIP catalogue record for this book is available from the British Library.

The publisher would like to thank the following for permission to reproduce their material.
Every care has been taken to trace copyright holders. However, if there have been
unintentional omissions or failure to trace copyright holders, we apologize and will,
if informed, endeavour to make corrections in any future edition.

(OFC = Outside Front Cover, OBC = Outside Back Cover, b = bottom, c = centre, l = left, r = right, t = top)

OFC, OBC all courtesy of Shutterstock; 2–3, 46–47 twobee/Shutterstock; 5, 10–11 (background) Kathriba/
Shutterstock; 8bl, 40–41bc Nate Allred/Shutterstock; 8cl swa182/Shutterstock; 8tl PetrP/Shutterstock;
8–9c Iakov Filimonov/Shutterstock; 8–9tc Maria Starovoytova/Shutterstock; 9bc, 14c (dam), 25cr 2009fotofriends/
Shutterstock; 9br, 30bl, 30bc Kichigin/Shutterstock; 9tl Tristan3D/Shutterstock; 10bl G. Brad Lewis/Science Photo
Library; 10tr IM_photo/Shutterstock; 10cr Brian A. Jackson/Shutterstock; 10–11bc Cordelia Molloy/Science Photo
Library; 11c cyo bo/Shutterstock; 11tl (bridge) Andrei Seleznev/Shutterstock; 11tl (joint) Spencer Grant/Science
Photo Library; 12l Duncan Shaw/Science Photo Library; 12tr Christopher Wood/Shutterstock; 12br Nature Picture
Library/Alamy; 13tl Jaromir Chalabala/Shutterstock; 13tr lightpoet/Shutterstock; 13c WENN Ltd/Alamy;
13b Bernhard Edmaier/Science Photo Library; 14–15tc Incredible Arctic/Shutterstock; 14bl, 40bl Footage.Pro/
Shutterstock; 14br Mint Images – Frans Lanting; 14cl Daniel Rose/Shutterstock; 14–15 (map) Stephen Marques/
Shutterstock; 15br Kevin Schafer/Corbis; 15cl Carolina K. Smith MD/Shutterstock; 15cr BMJ/Shutterstock;
15t jim kruger/Getty Images; 16bc Dr Jeremy Burgess/Science Photo Library; 16l Ashley Cooper pics/Alamy;
16tr CandyBox Images/Shutterstock; 17br The Curious Travelers/Shutterstock; 17c anyaivanova/Shutterstock;
17tl, 31tr Ria Novosti/Science Photo Library; 17tr karenfoleyphotography/Shutterstock.com; 18–19c Henrik
Sorensen; 18bl (truck) R.S.Jegg/Shutterstock; 18bl (ice) SOMMAI/Shutterstock; 18br lucvar/Shutterstock;
18cr Charles D. Winters/Science Photo Library; 18tl, 40–41tc M. Unal Ozmen/Shutterstock; 19bc INTERFOTO/
Alamy; 19bl Everett Collection Historical/Alamy; 19br, 24bl Mikkel Juul Jensen/Science Photo Library; 19t Buena
Vista Images; 19cr Wristify; 20–21 (sunset) Balashova Ekaterina/Shutterstock; 20br imageBROKER/Alamy;
21cl Library of Congress/Science Photo Library; 21tr westphalia; 22bl Doug Allan/Science Photo Library;
22br Nicolas Dubreuil/Look At Sciences/Science Photo Library; 22cr (icefish) British Antarctic Survey/Science Photo
Library; 22t fivepointsix/Shutterstock; 23cl Barcroft Media/Contributor/Getty Images; 23t (sea) AndreAnita/
Shutterstock; 23tr, 40–41tc (gull) Dmytro Pylypenko/Shutterstock; 23br Karim Agabi/Eurelios/Science Photo
Library; 24–25 (snow) Eugene Sergeev/Shutterstock; 24–25c (mammoth) Ozja/Shutterstock; 25br, 31tl Dr Juerg
Alean/Science Photo Library; 25tr Sheila Terry/Science Photo Library; 26br Topical Press Agency/Getty Images;
26l (yeti) Andreas Meyer/Shutterstock; 26l (trees) JeniFoto/Shutterstock; 26bl itakefotos4u/Shutterstock;
27c (trees) Shutterstock; 26cr (map) Stephen Marques/Shutterstock; 27bc Victorian Traditions/Shutterstock;
27l Andrey Yurlov/Shutterstock; 27tr, 41br Kachinadoll/Shutterstock; 28 RGB Ventures/SuperStock/Alamy;
28br Vienna Report Agency/Sygma/Corbis; 29t Niyazz/Shutterstock; 29cl AFP/Stringer/Getty Images; 29cr Danita
Delimont/Getty Images; 30br Taras Kushnir/Shutterstock; 30tc silver tiger/Shutterstock; 30tr Triff/Shutterstock;
31b JamesChen/Shutterstock; 32br, Rolf Kosecki/Corbis; 32l Ipatov/Shutterstock; 33r Greg Epperson/Shutterstock
(climber); 33r (diver) Kimmo Keskinen/Shutterstock; 33r (shovel racer) Lynn Eubank/Wikipedia; 33r (heli-skier)
Randy Lincks/Corbis; 33r (swimmer) Svetlana Yudina/Shutterstock; 33bl Mitrofanov Alexander/Shutterstock.com;
33tl Paolo Bona/Shutterstock.com; 34–35 (background) daizuoxin/Shutterstock; 34bl Feliks/Shutterstock;
34tr Marcel Jancovic/Shutterstock; 34br David Vaughan/Science Photo Library; 35b (icebreaker) Danita Delimont/
Alamy; 35b (ice) PHOTOCREO Michal Bednarek/Shutterstock; 35c Vladimir Melnikov/Shutterstock; 35t Louise
Murray/Alamy; 36br NASA/Science Photo Library; 36bl Detlev Van Ravenswaay/Science Photo Library;
36–37 (stars) McCarthy's PhotoWorks/Shutterstock; 37tl, 40–41tc (neptune) Georgios Kollidas/Shutterstock;
37c CHANARAT/Shutterstock; 37br Mark Garlick/Science Photo Library; 38cl MarcelClemens/Shutterstock;
38bl Eye of Science/Science Photo Library; 38–39c Aurora Photos/Alamy; 39cl deepspacedave/Shutterstock;
39tl Coprid/Shutterstock; 39br Cory Richards/National Geographic Society/Corbis; 40cl Tomo Jesenicnik/
Shutterstock; 41tr Khomulo Anna/Shutterstock; 41br (ice cubes) Valentyn Volkov/Shutterstock; 42–43 DarkBird/
Shutterstock; 44–45 Supertrooper/Shutterstock. All textures and design elements are courtesy of Shutterstock.

Contents

Cold, cold, cold!

It is a cold winter's day and the temperature outside is low. Your breath becomes visible as clouds of fog; you begin to shiver. The frost makes patterns on the windows and the snow glistens on the ground. But different people feel cold at different temperatures. While someone who lives in a warm country near the Equator may think that 0°C is cold, someone who lives in the north of Canada may not consider it really chilly until it reaches –20°C.

Cold describes something that is deprived of heat and has a low temperature. It's a word we use to discuss many aspects of the world around us. There are parts of our planet – the poles, some mountaintops – that are covered in snow and ice. In the depths of the oceans, fish move sluggishly through icy waters in the pitch black. But many humans, animals and plants have adapted to these cold places, using surprising and often inventive techniques for keeping warm.

The science of cold

Cold is an absence of warmth. You become cold when more heat leaves your body than you can replace. This may be because you are outside in winter without a scarf and gloves, or have gone swimming in chilly water. The cold causes materials to behave in interesting ways and this cold science has impressive applications.

CONDENSATION

As a gas cools, its particles move more slowly. At a particular point, the gas condenses to become a liquid. Condensation in the atmosphere happens when air is cooled to its dew point – for instance, when water in the air forms water droplets of dew on cold objects near the ground. Similarly, in a bathroom, steam from a bath or basin of hot water often condenses onto the cold windows, making them 'steam up'.

When hot lava from a volcano flows into the sea, the water boils. The steam condenses to form a mist of tiny droplets.

SUPERCOOLING

Supercooling happens when a liquid is chilled below its freezing point but still does not become solid. There are droplets of supercooled water in many cumulus clouds. If these droplets gather on a passing aeroplane, they may freeze and ice up the wings.

FREEZING

Different substances freeze at different temperatures. Water, for example, freezes at 0°C, mercury at −38.8°C, and nitrogen at −198°C (see page 18). This is because the molecules of the three substances are different. Some have weaker forces holding them together – in this case, mercury and nitrogen molecules have much weaker attractive forces than water molecules have.

GETTING SMALLER

Most materials contract, or get smaller, when they are cooled (the exception to this is ice, see page 12). This is because all the atoms are not moving about as much – they do not have as much kinetic energy. They move closer together and do not take up as much space.

Bridges, many buildings and railway lines have special joints fitted so the metal can expand in warm weather and contract in cold weather. If these joints were not used, the structures would buckle and collapse.

SUPERCONDUCTORS

These are extraordinary materials whose resistance drops to zero when they are cooled – which makes them excellent conductors of electricity. For example, there are two filters made of superconducting material in the Jodrell Bank radio telescope. They filter out atmospheric noise (signals from satellites and television receivers, for example) so that signals from space can be heard better.

In Japan, Maglev trains use superconducting electromagnetic coils to levitate approximately 10cm above their tracks.

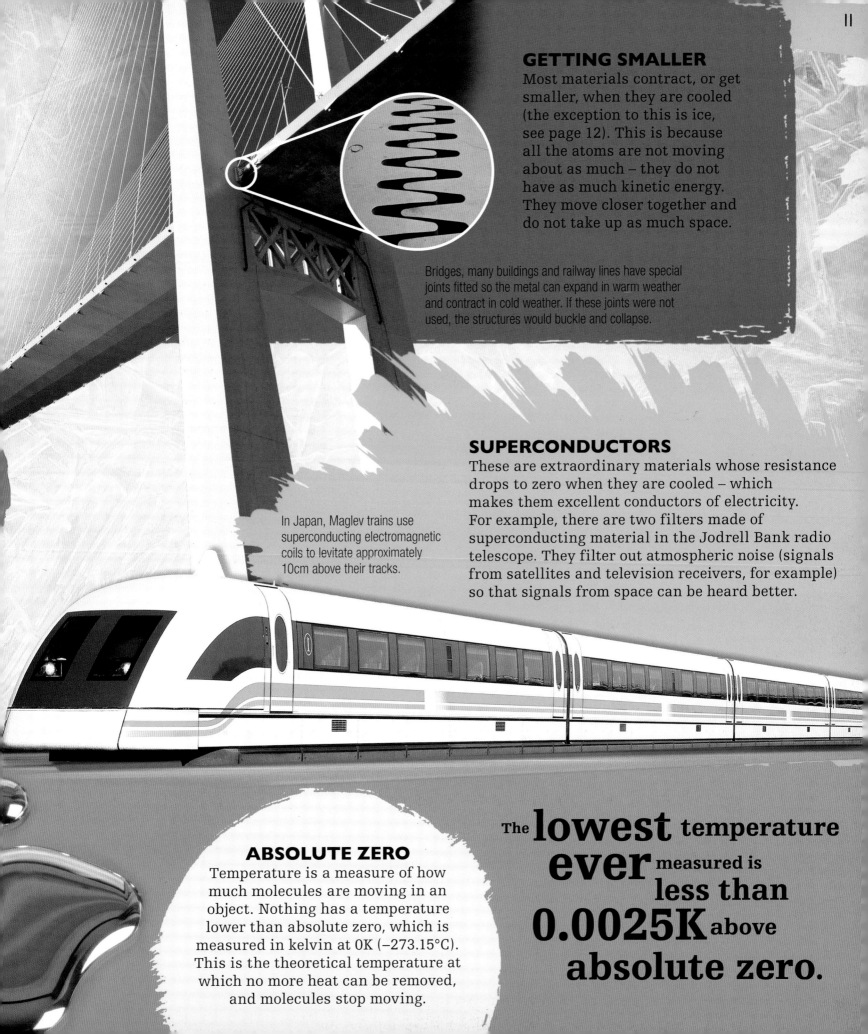

ABSOLUTE ZERO

Temperature is a measure of how much molecules are moving in an object. Nothing has a temperature lower than absolute zero, which is measured in kelvin at 0K (−273.15°C). This is the theoretical temperature at which no more heat can be removed, and molecules stop moving.

The **lowest** temperature **ever** measured is **less than 0.0025K** above **absolute zero.**

Ice cold

Ice is the solid, frozen form of water. It's cold, beautiful, slippery and sometimes deadly. It can be enormous – a glacier – or tiny – an ice crystal.

ICY WATERS

Most materials contract, or get smaller, as they cool down but ice behaves differently. Below 4°C, water starts to expand slightly until at 0°C it becomes ice. When water freezes, ice floats on the top, allowing water to stay liquid underneath.

Water that has salt in it can freeze too, and it also floats. But salt water does not freeze until it is much colder than fresh water: it needs to reach −2°C. The ice that forms is not salty, because the salt gets squeezed out.

ICED UP

When water gets colder, its molecules lose energy, move more slowly and begin to link up. When enough are linked, they form a rigid crystal structure with a pattern (see above)– this is ice. The molecules are now farther apart, so the ice is less dense and will float.

HOT ICE

Mt Erebus is the most active of Antarctica's volcanoes. Hot volcanic gases steam from a lava lake in its crater. They travel through cracks in the rocks around the summit to form the most extraordinary ice caves.

This ice cave is in the glacier that flows down Mt Erebus and out 11km into the sea off the coast of Antarctica.

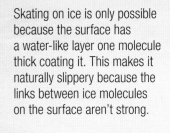

Skating on ice is only possible because the surface has a water-like layer one molecule thick coating it. This makes it naturally slippery because the links between ice molecules on the surface aren't strong.

These aircraft are being sprayed with antifreeze to remove ice before take-off. The antifreeze soaks deep into the ice, causing it to melt. It also prevents any refreezing during the flight.

DANGERS OF ICE

Ice can cause great damage – from aircraft wings icing up to frozen waterpipes bursting. It is possible to avoid disaster by spreading salt on icy roads, or by using antifreeze chemicals that lower the freezing point of the water by up to 37°C.

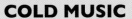

COLD MUSIC

You can carve musical instruments from blocks of ice cut from a frozen fjord and play them! The IceMusic Festival takes place in Geilo, Norway, every year and musicians from all over the world perform. The quality of the ice depends on the weather, so the sounds vary – dirt or bubbles in the ice dull the purity of the notes.

ICE SHEETS

These very large glaciers (see pages 28–29) cover vast areas. Today, there are only two ice sheets on Earth – Antarctica and Greenland. The preservation of this ice is vital to our survival – if the Greenland ice sheet melts, sea levels around the world would rise by about seven metres!

The **Antarctic ice sheet** contains **25 million km³** of **ice**.

The Greenland ice sheet covers the area surrounding the North Pole. Meeting the water, the ice sheet stretches over it to form an ice shelf. Parts of the shelf break off, forming icebergs.

Animals
in the cold

When it is winter in the north, the Arctic tern flies south – almost as far south as it's possible to go, all the way to Antarctica. To return home, it uses the steady southerly wind over the parts of the Atlantic Ocean to help it on its way.

ARCTIC TERN

Animals and plants are found all over the Earth, even in its coldest regions. Some spend their lives in icy conditions, while others live in places where the temperature changes greatly during a year. Over millions of years, the habits and bodies of living things have developed to help them survive.

NORTH AMERICAN BEAVER

Centuries ago, people had to store up food during the summer months to eat during the winter. Beavers also do this, building up supplies of tree bark as winter food. These caches, as they are called, are sometimes as much as 12m wide and 3m tall.

Like humans, beavers keep warm in winter by staying indoors. Sometimes, different beaver homes (called lodges) have connecting tunnels so the beavers can huddle together in the coldest weather.

EMPEROR PENGUIN

Young penguin chicks keep off the cold ground by sitting on their parent's feet.

Penguins have layers of fat and close-packed feathers to protect them from the sub-zero temperatures of Antarctica, but during blizzards even this isn't enough. So the penguins huddle together in enormous groups. The outer penguins are most exposed, so they take it in turns to swap places with ones from inside the group.

GREY WOLF

The difference in temperature between boiling water and your hand is about 70°C, which is about the same as the temperature difference between cold snow and a wolf's body. How does the wolf stand it? By sending very little blood to its paws, it allows them to cool gradually to near freezing point.

DORMOUSE

Some animals hibernate for weeks or months when it is cold. The dormouse eats as much as it can before hibernating, and has food stored for when it wakes. It spends more than half its life asleep.

WOOD FROG

Wood frogs have an amazing way of combating the cold. They can survive chilly winters by using chemicals produced by their liver as an antifreeze. Their skin and blood freeze, and their hearts and kidneys even shut down. When warmer weather returns, the frogs thaw and all their vital organs begin working again.

WHALES

Whales are mammals, just like humans. All mammals have warm blood, but whales live in water that is often around freezing. We keep heat in our bodies during freezing weather by wearing layers of clothes. Whales have thick layers of blubber under their skin that do the same job.

The blue whale is the largest creature that has ever lived.

People and the Cold

People are not equipped to deal with the cold. The human body needs to generate enough heat by burning food, and prevent the loss of that heat by wearing suitable clothing and finding shelter. However, the cold has encouraged many people to come up with clever inventions and creative ideas.

Every year there are stories of people being revived, even after several hours.

SNOW SLEEP

Cold is dangerous! You become hypothermic when your body temperature drops below 35°C – you cannot make decisions, you shiver violently and you get slower. Below 32°C, shivering stops because there is no energy to keep it going, and you become unconscious at around 30°C.

KEEPING WARM

There is nowhere on Earth colder than Antarctica (see pages 22–23). To combat the weather there, people wear many layers. The layer worn next to the skin is soft, comfortable material that pulls away moisture from the body so that it stays dry. Then there is a middle layer or layers made of wool or another natural fibre, which is topped by a waterproof and windproof breathable outer layer.

Materials such as Gore-tex (right) were invented to make waterproof layers for outdoor clothing. Gore-tex's membrane (yellow) has tiny pores that allow sweat from the body to pass through.

DID YOU KNOW?

Inside your brain is the hypothalamus, a tiny gland that acts as a thermostat when it senses your body temperature dropping. It is very sensitive to temperature change and is designed to protect your vital organs. It can do this in different ways:

- Sweating stops.
- Minute muscles under the skin contract, causing goosebumps.
- Shivering increases heat production in muscles.
- Blood flow to the skin is restricted to prevent heat loss.
- Fat is converted into energy inside cells, producing heat.

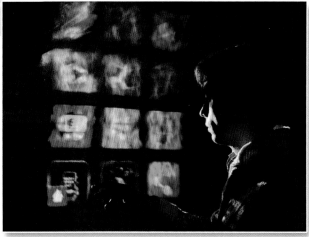

COLD 3D

A recent invention involves a floating touchscreen that uses a cold fog of ultra-fine water droplets to create an interactive display. 3D images are projected onto sheets of mist in which the cold water droplets are so tiny that they have hardly any moisture in them.

The user can use hand movements to interact with the images.

CRYOSTORAGE

Scientists use cryostorage – keeping materials at extremely low temperatures – to store materials, such as blood samples, DNA, and plant seeds or shoots, until they are needed. This prevents them from deteriorating so they will be fresh when scientific tests are conducted.

Research samples of DNA are preserved by freezing. Then they're thawed when needed for study in the lab.

BUILDING WITH ICE

It takes 1,000 tonnes of ice from the River Torne and 30,000 tonnes of 'snice', a mixture of snow and ice, to make the ICEHOTEL. This amazing hotel is built in the village of Jukkasjärvi, Sweden, every year to take guests from December to mid-April. One hundred people work on it from November onwards. Even the bedrooms and beds are made of ice (above).

ICE ART

In China, from the 17th century onwards, peasants made ice lanterns to use during the winter months. Holes were chiselled out of a lump of ice and candles inserted, and the lanterns became part of their festivals. Today, ice and snow sculpture is very popular in China with international competitions for ice artists.

The *creation* of **cold**

Making cold really means removing heat. It sounds easy, but it took centuries of experimenting before people learned how to build cooling machines that really worked. Now we use them to keep us cool, chill drinks, preserve food and even make snow.

Ice cream was an expensive treat in Europe and the USA in the 19th century. Only the wealthy could afford the ice houses that were needed to keep it cool.

LIQUID NITROGEN

An extremely cold fluid called liquid nitrogen (−198°C) can be used to freeze objects quickly. If you freeze a flower in this way it will maintain its shape, but it'll be so brittle that it's sure to smash into tiny pieces if dropped.

CONTROLLING COLD

As well as creating cold, we can control it. Pure water freezes at 0°C, but salty water freezes at a lower temperature. So, adding salt to ice that is at 0°C makes it melt. This is why salt is so useful for clearing ice from roads.

REFRIGERATION *Timeline*

Yakhchals *c.400BCE*
The world's first fridges were stone buildings called yakhchals. They had really thick walls. Ice was packed inside during the winter. In summer, water surrounding the walls kept the temperature low enough so that the ice wouldn't melt.

Yakhchal, Middle East

DESERT SNOW

Using huge, powerful air conditioners, freezers and snowmakers, indoor landscapes of snow and ice can be made anywhere – even in the middle of hot deserts. This artificial ski resort (left) is in Dubai, where the typical outside temperature is over 30°C.

COOL FACT

Wealthy people in hot countries had ceiling fans 200 years ago. They were powered by servants walking around in circles.

Dry ice is used at gigs to create dramatic effects.

Futuristic cooling system

DRY ICE

Liquids and gases turn to solids if they get cold enough. Dry ice is a solid version of the gas called carbon dioxide. It is so cold (about −80°C) that it chills the surrounding air very quickly. The water molecules in the air slow down and stick together to form millions of tiny droplets, looking like a dense cloud on the ground.

Hand-held coolers
Tomorrow
Air conditioners are really fridges that cool the air in humid rooms. Small versions work by passing electricity through metals. One day, we might be able to wear portable cooling devices!

Cutaway image of a modern fridge

Ice wagons *c.1850*
Before people could make ice, it was collected from chilly mountains or lakes instead. If customers could afford it, the ice was delivered to their homes in wagons.

Ice wagon, USA

Flame-driven fridges *c.1920s*
Scientists eventually learned how to create cold using electric refrigeration. But lots of homes had no electricity, so they powered early fridges with oil or gas.

Gas fridge, Germany

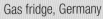

Modern fridges
Today
Refrigerant liquids are pumped around the pipes in a fridge. They absorb heat and become gases – this cools the fridge. Heat is then released and the whole process starts again.

Arctic chill

Our planet has two poles, one at the northern tip and one at the southern. The northern polar region is called the Arctic. It is a place of ice, snow and plunging temperatures.

THE NORTH POLE

An imaginary line around the northern polar area is called the Arctic Circle. It includes parts of America, Europe and Asia, as well as a huge area of frozen ocean with the North Pole at its centre. The North Pole itself is not in any country – it is considered part of international waters.

−40°C is the lowest temperature in the Arctic.

POLAR NIGHT

The town of Longyearbyen, Norway (right), is one of the most northerly towns in the world. Winters last for three months, are freezing and totally dark. This is because, in winter, the tilt of Earth as it orbits around the Sun means that the Arctic Circle gets no sunlight at all. The town is built on up to 40m of permafrost – soil that is permanently frozen all year round.

ARCTIC TOURISTS

The extreme landscape of the North Pole is a barren place. There's no land, just lots of ice. The polar ice floats – so if you put a marker down, it will only be on the North Pole for a moment before it drifts away.

Tourists travel to the North Pole by air. There's no sign to show where the pole is, so people use GPS to find the exact spot.

Peary, and his huskies, travelled from New York to Ellesmere Island by ship.

POLAR EXPLORERS

The North Pole is about 1,000km from land. It was first reached by US explorer Robert Peary in 1909. Peary travelled to an Arctic island by ship and then used huskies for his journey. He didn't have very good evidence to prove he'd made it to the pole, though. The first verified visit was made by Roald Amundsen and Umberto Nobile. They flew over it in an airship in 1926.

PERMAFROST

If you were to dig down into the soil in the Arctic, you would be able to go less than 1m before you struck permafrost – a mixture of soil, rocks and frozen water. The thickness of the permafrost varies from less than 1m to more than 1,500m. The brief summer sunlight cannot warm the ground deep enough to reach this layer and melt it, so some permafrost is actually thousands of years old.

North Pole ice can be up to 9m thick.

Antarctica

Antarctica is the coldest, highest and driest continent on Earth. Summer temperatures are about –20°C, and it can reach –60°C in winter. Its average height above sea level is 2,500m, and it has as little moisture as the world's hot deserts. It is an ice-covered wilderness where very few animals and plants are able to survive.

ICEFISH

The icefish, like many other fish in the Southern Ocean around Antarctica, produces antifreeze proteins to prevent ice crystals forming in its blood. These allow the fish to survive in temperatures that can drop to –1.9°C, the freezing point of seawater.

HARD GROWTH

Few plants can grow in Antarctica. Its freezing conditions, poor soil, lack of moisture and very little sunlight mean that only the toughest plants can survive there. The majority are lichens, mosses, liverworts and algae.

Emperor penguins spend their entire lives in Antarctica, and are the only animals to live on the open ice during the winter. When they have bred, the female leaves to hunt while the male stands for up to 70 days with the egg balanced on his feet in a warm brood pouch. This happens despite biting winds of –60°C and blizzards that reach 200km/h.

Some algae will even grow on and under the Antarctic ice.

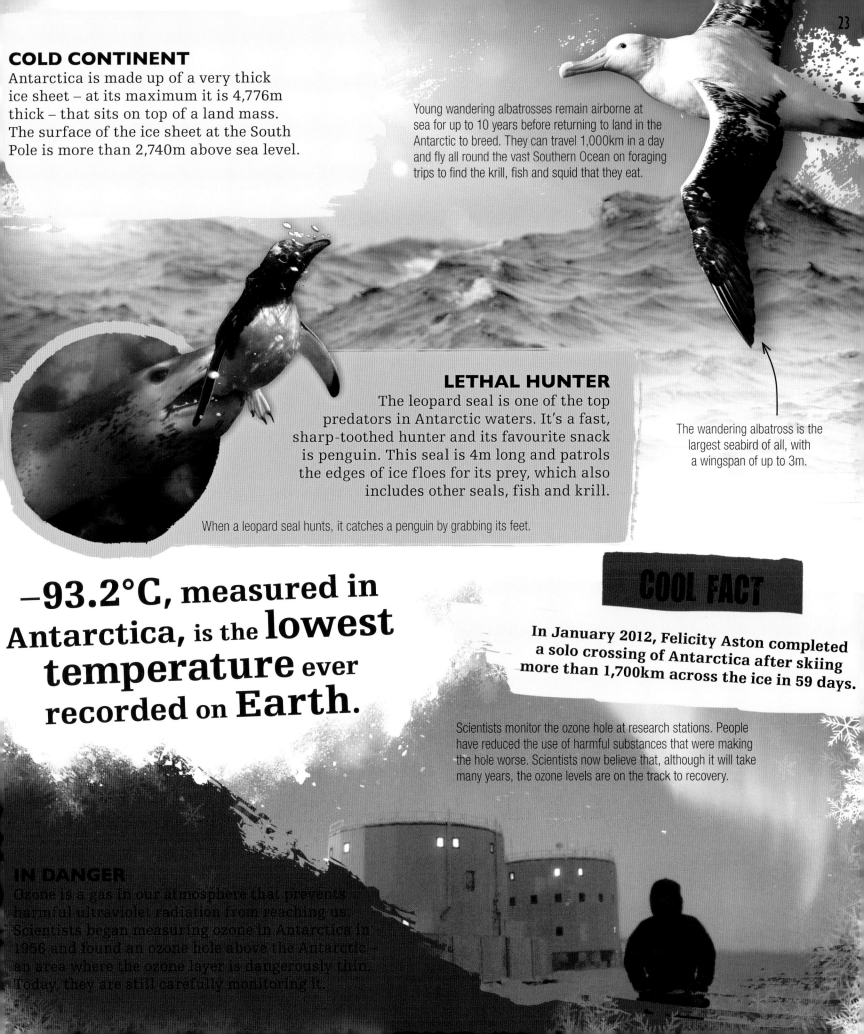

COLD CONTINENT

Antarctica is made up of a very thick ice sheet – at its maximum it is 4,776m thick – that sits on top of a land mass. The surface of the ice sheet at the South Pole is more than 2,740m above sea level.

Young wandering albatrosses remain airborne at sea for up to 10 years before returning to land in the Antarctic to breed. They can travel 1,000km in a day and fly all round the vast Southern Ocean on foraging trips to find the krill, fish and squid that they eat.

LETHAL HUNTER

The leopard seal is one of the top predators in Antarctic waters. It's a fast, sharp-toothed hunter and its favourite snack is penguin. This seal is 4m long and patrols the edges of ice floes for its prey, which also includes other seals, fish and krill.

When a leopard seal hunts, it catches a penguin by grabbing its feet.

The wandering albatross is the largest seabird of all, with a wingspan of up to 3m.

−93.2°C, measured in Antarctica, is the lowest temperature ever recorded on Earth.

COOL FACT

In January 2012, Felicity Aston completed a solo crossing of Antarctica after skiing more than 1,700km across the ice in 59 days.

Scientists monitor the ozone hole at research stations. People have reduced the use of harmful substances that were making the hole worse. Scientists now believe that, although it will take many years, the ozone levels are on the track to recovery.

IN DANGER

Ozone is a gas in our atmosphere that prevents harmful ultraviolet radiation from reaching us. Scientists began measuring ozone in Antarctica in 1956 and found an ozone hole above the Antarctic – an area where the ozone layer is dangerously thin. Today, they are still carefully monitoring it.

Ice ages

In an ice age, temperatures across the world get very low and enormous glaciers can cover whole countries or continents. There have been at least five major ice ages in Earth's history. The earliest was 2.4 billion years ago, and the latest began 2.58 million years ago and is continuing today!

WHAT CAUSES AN ICE AGE?

There are different theories about how ice ages begin:

- There are changes in Earth's orbit that increase the distance between Earth and the Sun, so Earth becomes colder.
- Not as much energy in the form of sunlight is coming from the Sun.
- There are low levels of greenhouse gases, such as carbon dioxide, in Earth's atmosphere.
- There are changes in ocean currents that cause ice sheets to build up.

Ice has covered most of the planet three times in Earth's history.

SNOWBALL EARTH

Some scientists think that during the Cryogenian Ice Age, about 650 million years ago, the polar ice sheets grew and met at the Equator. Snow and ice covered all of the Earth's land and oceans. The climate during this 'snowball' period would have been like that on Mars (see page 36).

ICE AGE SURVIVAL

From 1.8 million years ago to 11,700 years ago, glaciers covered large areas of Earth. Winter temperatures were up to 20°C lower than today. It was also drier because most of the world's water was locked up in ice sheets, so deserts expanded.

Between around 1350 and 1850, temperatures plummeted. The result was that Europe and North America had much colder winters than normal. Some were so cold that frost fairs could be held on frozen rivers. People call this period the Little Ice Age. The fair shown in this painting was held for two months in the winter of 1683–4 on the River Thames in London.

Large fur-covered animals evolved to survive the freezing conditions. Despite the ice and snow, mammoths ate small flowering plants very like the ones that flourish on mountaintops today.

TODAY'S ICE AGE

We live in the Quaternary Ice Age. Our climate today is one of the warm intervals between periods of glaciation that began about 11,000 years ago. Since then, glaciers have advanced and retreated more than 20 times. There are still ice sheets over Greenland, the Arctic and Antarctica (see pages 13 and 22–23).

The Athabasca Glacier is at the edge of the Columbia Icefield in the Canadian Rockies. It is currently retreating at a rate of 5m per year, and over the last 125 years has lost half its volume.

DID YOU KNOW?

Ice ages can last for millions or tens of millions of years. Swiss-born American scientist Louis Agassiz (1807–73) proved that glaciers (see page 28) advanced and retreated over time by studying the movements of glaciers in Switzerland.

Agassiz proved that glaciers move. He examined erratics – rocks that are carried away by glaciers and deposited in areas with different geologies.

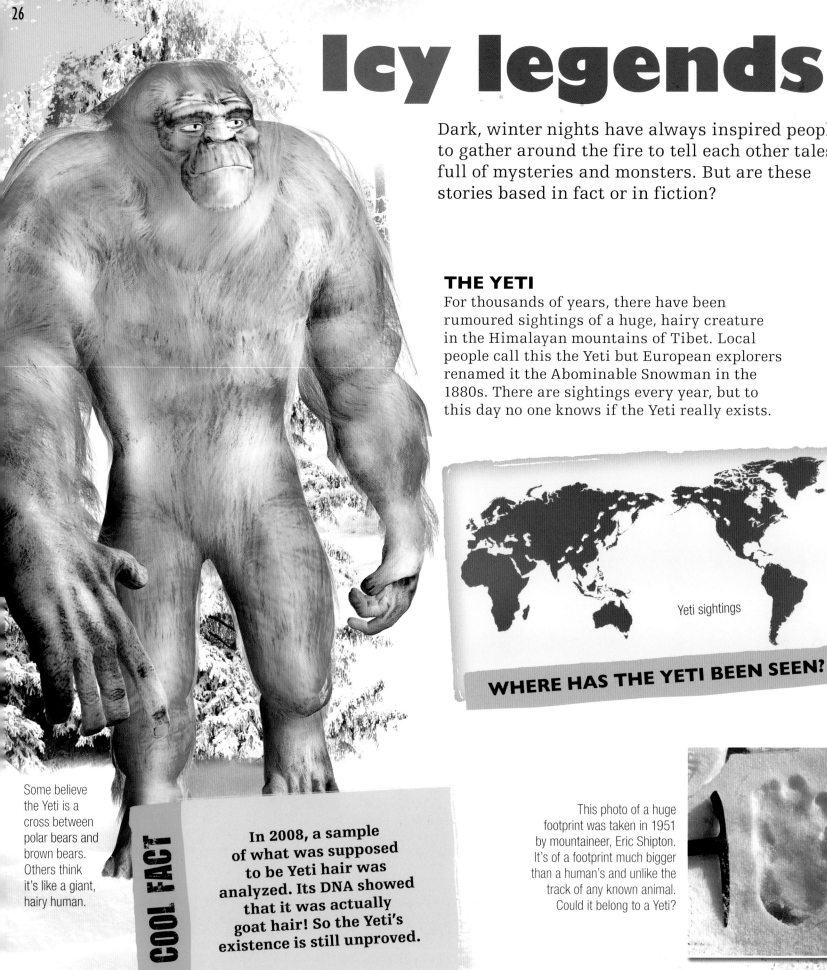

Icy legends

Dark, winter nights have always inspired people to gather around the fire to tell each other tales full of mysteries and monsters. But are these stories based in fact or in fiction?

THE YETI

For thousands of years, there have been rumoured sightings of a huge, hairy creature in the Himalayan mountains of Tibet. Local people call this the Yeti but European explorers renamed it the Abominable Snowman in the 1880s. There are sightings every year, but to this day no one knows if the Yeti really exists.

Yeti sightings

WHERE HAS THE YETI BEEN SEEN?

Some believe the Yeti is a cross between polar bears and brown bears. Others think it's like a giant, hairy human.

COOL FACT

In 2008, a sample of what was supposed to be Yeti hair was analyzed. Its DNA showed that it was actually goat hair! So the Yeti's existence is still unproved.

This photo of a huge footprint was taken in 1951 by mountaineer, Eric Shipton. It's of a footprint much bigger than a human's and unlike the track of any known animal. Could it belong to a Yeti?

JACK FROST

Jack Frost is a mischievous spirit who's meant to control ice and snow. According to legend, he is responsible for the ice patterns on windows. A nasty pinch from him is said to make people shivery and even ill.

NANOOK – THE GREAT BEAR

The Inuit are native peoples in Arctic parts of North America and Greenland, who once hunted polar bears for meat and furs. They believed that one bear, called Nanook, was mighty and that he was responsible for the success of hunts. They thought all polar bears were magical, so hunters would offer knives as gifts to please the spirits of slain bears.

COOL FACT

Japanese legends tell of Yuki-onna, the Snow Woman, who can float across the snow leaving no footprints. She is said to freeze lost travellers with her icy breath.

SANTA CLAUS

Santa Claus is said to fly around the world on Christmas Eve delivering gifts to children. The earliest-known version of this festive figure was a real gift-giving Greek bishop called Nicholas. He was born at the end of the 3rd century and was named a saint 200 years later. For years, Santa Claus was depicted dressed in green. He came to be depicted in red because of an illustrated 19th-century poem, *A Visit from Saint Nicholas*.

Rivers of ice

Glaciers are great frozen rivers that move extremely slowly downhill towards the sea. They grind away even the hardest rocks, dragging their remains along with them. When the glaciers reach lower, warmer areas, the ice melts.

A glacier moves a distance of about one metre per year.

The highest part of a glacier is constantly renewed as fresh snow falls on the surface.

The dark lines are streams of mud and rock, scraped by the glacier ice as it flows slowly past.

Valley shredded by grinding ice.

Glaciers store about **75%** of the world's fresh water.

ÖTZI
While bringing frozen corpses back to life is still science fiction, some glaciers do contain them. One ice mummy, Ötzi the Iceman, was found near the Similaun mountain on the border between Austria and Italy. He is 5,300 years old.

Only a small amount of any iceberg is visible above sea level. A staggering 90% of its volume lies hidden below the water.

ICE GIANT

One of the largest icebergs in the world floats in the Southern Ocean off Antarctica, it's named B31. At 660km^2 in area and 500m thick, it is a third the size of London. Icebergs and other huge chunks of ice break off from glaciers or ice sheets (see page 13) when they meet the ocean in a process called calving.

LIFE OF AN ICEBERG

Once an iceberg calves, it usually lasts for about three to six years. This time may be shorter if the iceberg floats into warmer water, or very much longer if it does not – some may last 50 years or more.

TITANIC

On 14 April 1912, the steamship *Titanic* struck an iceberg in the northern Atlantic, ripping a 90m gash in its hull. Three hours later, the ship, and more than 1,500 of its crew and passengers, were gone.

Between **10,000** and **15,000** icebergs are **calved** each year.

Frost and Snow

In many parts of the world, winter brings freezing temperatures, snow and ice. For some it is the signal for having fun, but for others cold weather brings storms and danger.

WINTRY WEATHER

Earth travels around the Sun every year. Our planet is tilted on its axis so the weather changes dramatically through the year in some countries. When areas are tilted away from the Sun, they get colder temperatures – winter. This is because sunlight is striking the surface at a low angle and the areas receive less sunlight.

BLIZZARDS

These violent snowstorms have very strong winds that travel at more than 55km/h. They happen when there is very cold air at ground level, mixed with howling winds and blowing snow. Icy winds can make chilly air feel even colder.

The 2011 US **Groundhog Day Blizzard** stretched over **3,200km** and **22 states**.

The blowing snow can cause dangerous whiteouts, with people becoming disoriented and unable to see anything.

A snowflake is six-pointed and made of up to 200 ice crystals. Snowflakes form around tiny bits of dirt, in clouds below −15°C. As the flakes grow, they get heavier and fall to the ground.

RIME ICE

This kind of ice forms when tiny droplets of extremely cold water freeze instantly on contact with a cold vertical surface. Rime ice is usually only found at high altitudes and is quite delicate, shattering easily when touched.

This rime ice has formed in long plumes called 'frost feathers' on pillars at a meteorological station high up in the Swiss Alps.

These extraordinary light pillars appear to beam upwards from the city of Naberezhnye Chelny, Russia. In fact, the pillars are being reflected down from ice crystals that are about halfway between the camera and city's lights.

FROST

White frost crystals build up because water vapour from the air becomes solid when the temperature goes below freezing. Ice looks very pretty when it glitters in the sunlight, but it can be very damaging to plants and crops.

Frost can crack rocks! This granite rock has been broken by water that has frozen and thawed repeatedly.

FROST QUAKES

On Christmas Eve 2013, people in Toronto, Canada, were awoken by several loud booms. Scientists say this was cryoseism, or a frost quake. Frost quakes happen when a sudden freezing puts stress on the ground and soil. The rock cracks, creating a loud sound and sometimes shaking the surface.

Cold sports

For some people, a chilly day means difficult journeys or staying indoors. But others reach for their skates or skis and rush outside. Enthusiasts even go to far-off snowy places in search of more action. Welcome to the chilly world of cold sports.

SNOWBOARDING

The first specially made snowboard was built by US inventor Sherman Poppen, in 1965. He made it as a toy for his daughter. Soon his boards were so popular he had to open a factory to meet public demand. At that time, snowboarding was called snurfing.

The world speed snowboarding record is 201km/h. It was set by Australian boarder Darren Powell at *Les Arcs* resort in France, in 1999.

Early snowboards were made by fastening two skis together.

BOBSLED

Bobsled teams ride aerodynamic sleds along icy tracks, competing to achieve the fastest time. The most famous was perhaps the 1988 Jamaican team. Living in a hot country, they had little practice and even had to borrow a sled. Their story inspired the film *Cool Runnings*.

Bobsleds often travel at over 120km/h.

ICE SKATING

Skaters glide along the ice elegantly and quickly, whether they figure or speed skate. In 2006, Natalia Kanounnikova set the record for the fastest spin on ice skates. She completed 308 turns in one minute.

These Olympic relay speed skaters can reach speeds of 60km/h.

TOP FIVE
CRAZY CHILLY SPORTS

There is no shortage of weird sports in the world, and some of the chillier ones are odder than most.

1 Scrambling up the surfaces of frozen waterfalls is called ice climbing.

2 In full scuba gear, ice divers plummet into frozen lakes through holes carved in the ice.

3 Think sledding is too tame? Shovel racing is similar, but a large shovel is used instead of a sled.

4 Heli-skiing fanatics hop out of hovering helicopters before darting down steep mountainsides. This allows them to reach untouched slopes.

5 Is an indoor pool too cosy? Imagine ice swimming in part-frozen lakes, without wearing any protective gear.

COOL FACT

At the first Winter Olympics, held in 1924, events included skating and military patrolling in the snow. Modern events now include snowboard slopestyle competitions, during which athletes perform jumps and stunts.

ICE HOCKEY

Each ice hockey team tries to get its puck into its opponent's goal. The pucks are made of rubber and fly along the ice at up to 190km/h. Early pucks probably moved more slowly, they were made from frozen cow dung!

Ice hockey is a contact sport so players are covered from head to toe in protective gear.

Vehicles
in the cold

There are more than 370,000km of snowmobile trails in the USA and Canada alone.

In the coldest places on Earth, even vehicles have a tough time. They need to be able to move over or through snow, ice and slush, and to protect their occupants in freezing conditions.

SNOWMOBILE

Although these vehicles were first designed for the military, today they are used for sport and competition all over the world. Tracks spread a snowmobile's weight over a greater surface area, which prevents it sinking into the snowy terrain.

The Autosub6000 can travel up to 1,000km and reach depths of 6,000m.

AUTOSUB

Autonomous Underwater Vehicles (AUVs) are robot submarines that are used to explore the Arctic and Antarctic. They operate under glaciers and sea ice and have even helped scientists map the seabed. They are also used to study creatures living at such freezing depths.

Skiers are able to zoom over snow because piste bashers have been at work. They move and flatten powdery snow and slush to create smooth pistes and trails. They have wide tracks and often tow special machinery to smooth the path behind them.

AIRBOAT

When sea ice is melting in the Arctic, it is too dangerous to use normal boats or snowmobiles. Instead, people drive special flat-bottomed boats powered by large above-water propellers to move people and goods across water or ice. These sturdy, adaptable vehicles are also used for search and rescue missions.

This airboat is towing a boat near Baffin Island, off the coast of Canada.

SLEDS AND SLEDGES

Wooden sleds or sledges were first used 9,000 years ago by people living on the edge of the Arctic Circle. They have been popular for travelling and moving goods through snowy regions ever since (see pages 20–21). Sledding is now a popular winter sport.

Sleds can be moved by a person alone, but are often pulled by teams of reindeer or dogs.

ICEBREAKER

If ships get trapped in hull-crushing sea ice, icebreakers come to the rescue. These vessels either have sharply pointed bows that cut through ice like knives or are large enough to ride up on top of the ice and smash down to break it.

The Russian icebreaker *Sovietsky Soyuz* smashes down through the frozen ice.

Cold worlds

There is no air in space, so there is no heat conduction or convection. Heat is only transferred when light from the Sun strikes an object. Planets and other space objects that are distant from the Sun do not get much sunlight and have chilly climates. These are cold worlds.

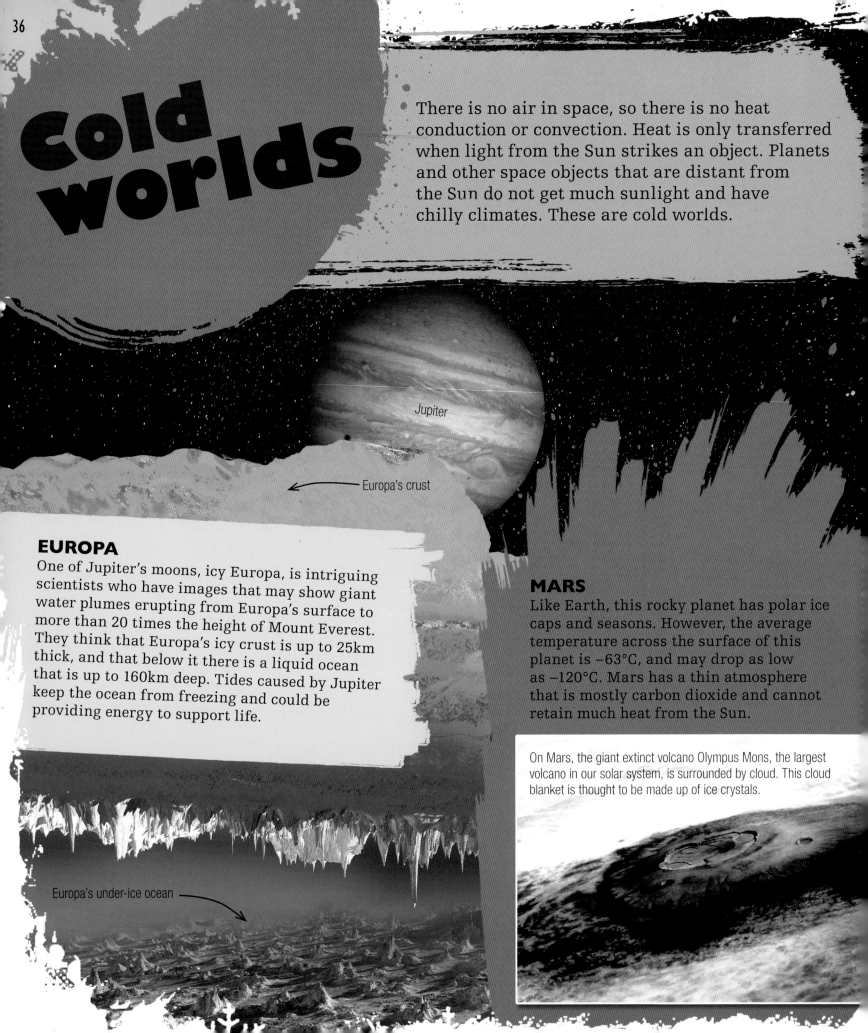

Jupiter

Europa's crust

EUROPA

One of Jupiter's moons, icy Europa, is intriguing scientists who have images that may show giant water plumes erupting from Europa's surface to more than 20 times the height of Mount Everest. They think that Europa's icy crust is up to 25km thick, and that below it there is a liquid ocean that is up to 160km deep. Tides caused by Jupiter keep the ocean from freezing and could be providing energy to support life.

MARS

Like Earth, this rocky planet has polar ice caps and seasons. However, the average temperature across the surface of this planet is −63°C, and may drop as low as −120°C. Mars has a thin atmosphere that is mostly carbon dioxide and cannot retain much heat from the Sun.

On Mars, the giant extinct volcano Olympus Mons, the largest volcano in our solar system, is surrounded by cloud. This cloud blanket is thought to be made up of ice crystals.

Europa's under-ice ocean

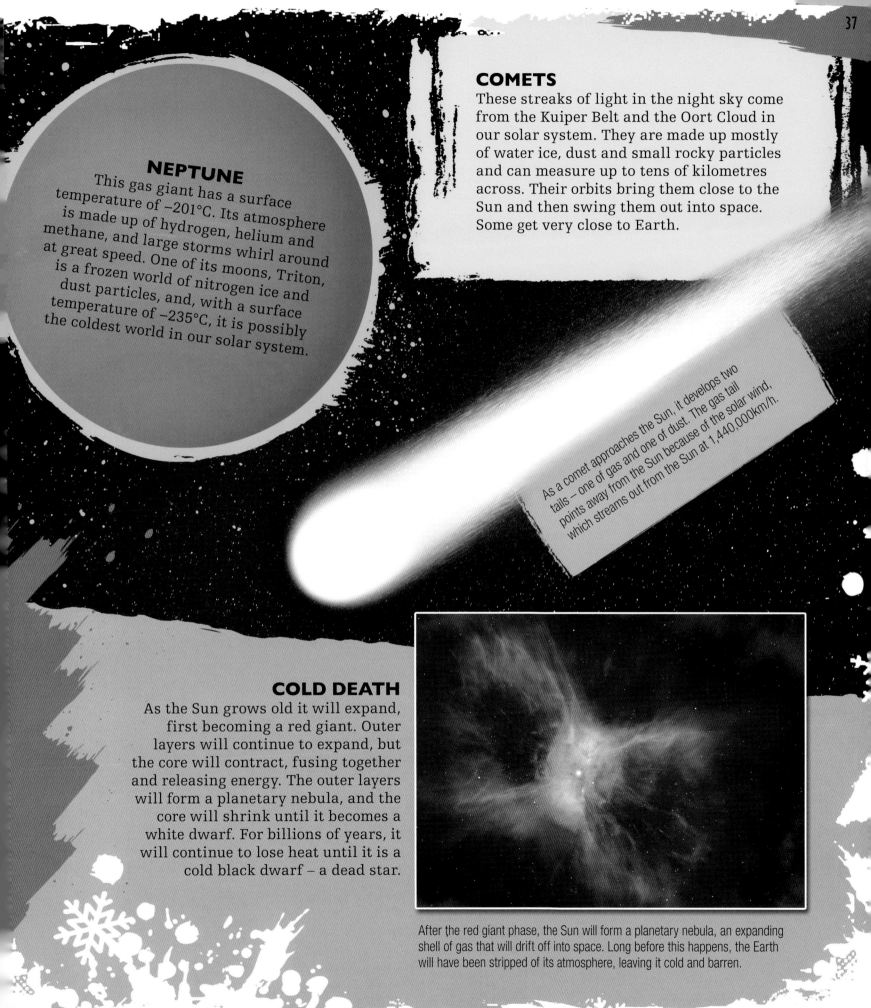

NEPTUNE

This gas giant has a surface temperature of −201°C. Its atmosphere is made up of hydrogen, helium and methane, and large storms whirl around at great speed. One of its moons, Triton, is a frozen world of nitrogen ice and dust particles, and, with a surface temperature of −235°C, it is possibly the coldest world in our solar system.

COMETS

These streaks of light in the night sky come from the Kuiper Belt and the Oort Cloud in our solar system. They are made up mostly of water ice, dust and small rocky particles and can measure up to tens of kilometres across. Their orbits bring them close to the Sun and then swing them out into space. Some get very close to Earth.

As a comet approaches the Sun, it develops two tails – one of gas and one of dust. The gas tail points away from the Sun because of the solar wind, which streams out from the Sun at 1,440,000km/h.

COLD DEATH

As the Sun grows old it will expand, first becoming a red giant. Outer layers will continue to expand, but the core will contract, fusing together and releasing energy. The outer layers will form a planetary nebula, and the core will shrink until it becomes a white dwarf. For billions of years, it will continue to lose heat until it is a cold black dwarf – a dead star.

After the red giant phase, the Sun will form a planetary nebula, an expanding shell of gas that will drift off into space. Long before this happens, the Earth will have been stripped of its atmosphere, leaving it cold and barren.

Strange **but true**

So cold is all around you – it gives you goosebumps, causes snow to fall and creates frozen rivers of ice. Here are some of the more extraordinary ways in which cold affects people and other living things on our planet.

IS IT A STAR?
If you are looking up at the night sky and spot a bright shooting star with a curly tail, this may be frozen urine and wastewater being dumped from the International Space Station.

GIANT SNOWWOMAN
In February 2008, the residents of Bethel, Maine, USA, built a snowwoman that was an amazing 37.21m tall.

The huge snowwoman didn't melt away until July 2008.

EXTREME SURVIVAL
A species of the micro-animal with eight legs, called a tardigrade or water bear, has been found in Antarctica. Tardigrades are less than one millimetre long, but are able to withstand extreme environments.

Tardigrades are the only creatures that can survive in the vacuum of space.

People with chionophobia are afraid of snow. A forecast of an approaching snowstorm can cause them to have panic attacks. Sufferers will not go out in snowy conditions for fear they might get stranded.

If the **ice** in all the **glaciers** and **ice sheets** melted, Earth's **sea level** would rise by **80m**.

Some search and rescue dogs, such as St Bernards and German Shepherds, can smell people who are buried under metres of snow. They are often used to look for survivors of avalanches.

DID YOU KNOW?

When film crews are recording summer scenes in winter, actors are given ice cubes to suck just before the cameras roll. The ice cools their mouths so that their breath does not condense in the cold air.

FROSTY FEELINGS

The earliest stages of frostbite are known as frostnip; symptoms include itchy, red skin and numbness. Frostnip doesn't permanently damage the skin but it can progress to frostbite. In extreme cases, fingers and toes might need to be amputated because of severe damage to the tissues.

Once rescued, frostbite victims need to be carefully warmed up again to get back to the correct body temperature.

Cold quiz

Now you have found out what makes you shiver and shake, you can test your knowledge with the coolest of quizzes!

1 Which famous ship hit an iceberg and then sank?

2 At what temperature does water freeze?

3 Which is the coldest world in our solar system?

4 What is ice?

5 Where on Earth are the lowest temperatures recorded?

6 How does a whale keep warm?

7 What is permafrost?

8 What gas is used to make dry ice?

9 What is the name of the present ice age?

10 How many points does a snowflake have?

11 What snow vehicle was first designed for the military?

EXTRA TOUGH QUESTIONS:

12 Why does ice float?

13 What is a dew point?

14 What piece of equipment is used look at the seabed under ice?

15 Which part of your body controls temperature?

16 What is cryoseism?

17 At what temperatures do humans become hypothermic?

1. *Titanic* (see p.29). **2.** 0°C (see p.10 and p.18). **3.** Neptune's moon Triton (see p.37). **4.** The frozen form of water (see p.12). **5.** Antarctica (see pp.22–23). **6.** By having thick layers of blubber (see p.15). **7.** Soil that is permanently frozen (see p.21). **8.** Carbon dioxide (see p.19). **9.** The Quaternary Ice Age (see p.25). **10.** Six (see p.30). **11.** The snowmobile (see p.34). **12.** Because it is less dense than water (see p.12). **13.** When water forms water droplets on objects near the ground (see p.10). **14.** An Autosub (see. p.34). **15.** The hypothalamus (see p.16). **16.** A frost quake (see p.31). **17.** Below 35°C (see p.16).

Websites and further reading

Explore these websites and visit the venues for more information about the frosty topics you have been reading about in the book.

- Water and air at Magna Science Adventure Centre, Sheffield: www.visitmagna.co.uk/science

- The ice moon Europa and other cold planets at the National Space Centre, Leicester: www.spacecentre.co.uk

- Natural recycling processes at the Bristol Science Centre, Bristol: www.at-bristol.org.uk/whatshere.html

- Water freezing and 'icy bodies' at the Launchpad in the Science Museum, London: www.sciencemuseum.org.uk/visitmuseum/plan_your_visit/exhibitions/launchpad. aspx?keywords=launchpad

- Polar explorers at the Scott Polar Research Institute, Cambridge: www.spri.cam.ac.uk/museum

- The extinction of ice age mammals at the Natural History Museum, London: www.nhm.ac.uk/visit-us/galleries/blue-zone/mammals/index.html

Here are some cool books for you to explore:

- *100 Science Experiments* by Georgina Andrews, Usborne Publishing 2012

- *Arctic and Antarctic*, Dorling Kindersley 2012

- *Mountain Climbing for Kids* by Steffen Kjaer, Alpine Avenue Books 2012

- *Space Encyclopedia* by David A. Aguilar, National Geographic Kids 2013

- *They Came From Beneath the Ice* by William J. Smith, lulu.com 2013

- *The Abominable Snow Kid* by Sean O'Reilly, Raintree 2014

Glossary

aerodynamics
The study of how air passes over and around objects. Aerodynamic design means that aircraft and cars move through air more smoothly.

algae
Simple plants that have no true roots or flowers.

altitude
The height of something, such as a mountain or aeroplane, above sea level on Earth.

atmosphere
The layer of mixed gases surrounding planet Earth.

atom
A tiny particle of matter, consisting of protons, neutrons and electrons. Atoms are the smallest particles that can take part in a chemical reaction.

axis
An imaginary straight line from the top to the bottom of a spinning object, such as Earth. The object turns or rotates around the line.

blizzard
A snowstorm blown by a very strong, very cold wind.

climate
The long-term or average weather of an area.

condense
To turn from a gas into a liquid. Water vapour condenses to become water and ice.

conductor
A material that conducts electricity or heat.

contract
To become smaller or shrink in size.

dense
Describes how heavy an object feels. The heavier an object's atoms, or the more tightly packed they are, the denser an object is.

dew point
The temperature at which air contains so much water vapour that it cannot hold any more and dew begins to form.

electromagnetic
Describes a type of magnet that can be switched on and off. When it is turned on, electricity flows through a coil of wire, creating a magnetic field.

extinct
No longer in existence.

fjord
A long, narrow place where the sea runs between high cliffs. Fjords usually form where sea water flows into valleys carved out by glaciers near the coast.

glaciation
The freezing of an area so that it is covered with ice or glaciers.

glacier
A slowly moving mass of ice that is caused by packed snow in an area increasing in size faster than it melts.

gravity
The force that pulls objects together. Gravity causes objects to be pulled towards a planet.

greenhouse gas
Any gas in the atmosphere that plays a part in the greenhouse effect – the trapping of heat by gases in a planet's atmosphere. The most important greenhouse gases are carbon dioxide and water vapour.

hibernate
To sleep deeply or stay still during the winter months. Animals hibernate so that they can survive cold weather.

hypothermic
Having an abnormally low body temperature, caused by exposure to cold weather.

ice floe
A floating piece of sea ice found in the Arctic or Antarctic.

iceberg
A large floating piece of ice that has broken off a glacier and is carried out to sea. Most of the ice is under the surface of the water.

kelvin
A temperature scale in which the lowest temperature possible is zero.

kinetic energy
The amount of work an object can do as a result of its motion. The kinetic energy of a moving object depends on its mass and how fast it is moving.

moisture
Water that is present in the air as tiny droplets.

molecule
A chemical unit made up of two or more atoms joined together.

nebula
A cloud of gas and dust in space.

orbit
To travel in a curved path around a body in space. Earth orbits the Sun.

ozone
A form of oxygen, this gas is found in Earth's atmosphere in minute quantities. It absorbs ultraviolet rays in the upper atmosphere and prevents them from reaching Earth's surface.

particle
A tiny piece of solid matter.

resistance
The extent to which something can slow down movement or electrical current.

satellite
An object that orbits a planet or another body. Communications satellites relay TV pictures around Earth.

temperature
The measure of how hot or cold something is. Thermometers are used to measure temperature in degrees.

thawed
Raised the temperature of something above its freezing point so that it becomes liquid. When ice thaws, it becomes water.

water vapour
Water in its gas form. The atmosphere contains water vapour.

Index